Yoyo Tricks for Kids

Including the EASIEST and SIMPLEST Yoyo Tricks to Become a Master

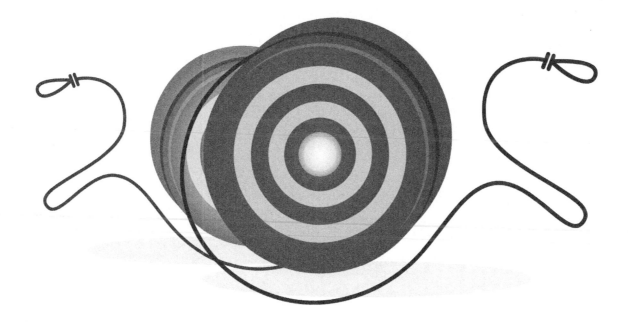

Charlotte Gibbs

SPECIAL BONUS!

Want These 2 Books For <u>FREE</u>?

 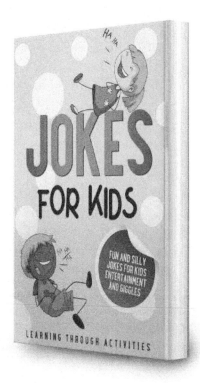

Get **<u>FREE</u>**, unlimited access to these and all of our new kids books by joining our community!

Scan W/ Your Camera To Join!

Table of Contents

 Introduction

Yoyos may be the most fun toy in the world because they're not just a toy, they're much more than that. Yoyos are a skill you can develop and perfect, you can learn dozens, hundreds of tricks to impress your friends and family. The possibilities of yoyos are endless!

Like action figures, dolls, building blocks… it's fun to play with yoyos and let your imagination run wild, but with yoyos you'll get better the more you practice and you'll be able to do more and more amazing tricks.

Some people practice hours and hours every day until they become authentic yoyo professionals and do absolutely beautiful tricks. But don't think about that right now, at the end of the day the main goal of yoyos is to be fun and have a great time with your friends, family or even on your own.

If you're looking to learn from scratch what a yoyo is, what types of yoyos there are, how to hold it well and a few tricks, this is your book! This is the perfect book to start your yoyo discovery journey, it's a whole world!

Like any new skill, it can be a little hard at first to understand and get your yoyo to work, but don't worry, you've got this! You may not get some moves right on the first try, but remember: practice makes perfect. I'm sure that little by little you will conquer each and every one of the tricks that you'll learn later in this book.

If you've played with a yoyo before, you might want to skip the first few sections, but I still recommend you take a look at them before moving on. And if you've never used one, don't worry! Here you will find all the information you need to get started: how to hold it, wind it and even throw it for the first time. Once you know how to do these things, and only when you feel confident to go ahead, you can learn a series of tricks from simpler to more complicated to blow your friends and family's minds.

One last tip: don't skip sections if you're not sure you know how to do it right and have practiced enough. I know it can get a bit boring sometimes, but if you try more difficult tricks without mastering the simpler ones you can get them wrong and feel a little frustrated, so don't take shortcuts!

That being said… Ready to enter the world of yo-yos and have a super good time learning this new skill with this cool toy? Let's go!

Choosing a Yoyo

I know that all yoyos look almost the same and it can be a bit complicated to choose the right one for you if you don't know what differences there are between them. That's why in this section you're going to see what types of yoyos there are and their differences, what shapes they have or what is the right length of the string for you.

Starting with the wrong yoyo can make it a bit more difficult for you to learn this new skill, so pay attention so you can decide which yoyo you need or you can identify it if you already have one.

Yoyos are made of a small bar attached to two disks of different materials, one on each side, with a gap between them. The other element of a yoyo is the string that's tied around that bar in the gap between the disks and to the middle finger of your hand at its other end. Well, depending on the shape of the disks and the size of the gap between them, as well as the way the yoyo behaves when you pull the thread, you will have a lot of different types of yoyos.

Types of Yoyos

There are two types of yoyos depending on what they do when you tug on the string: responsive and unresponsive yoyos. Long story short, a responsive yoyo is a yoyo that returns to your hand when you tug on the string, and an unresponsive yoyo won't return to your hand when you tug on it.

Responsive Yoyo

Responsive yoyos are those that quickly go back to your hand with a simple tug on the string. The tricks that you can do with a responsive yoyo are much more limited than the tricks you can do with an unresponsive yoyo, but they're a better option for beginners.

It's easier to learn how a yoyo works using a responsive yoyo because you'll have to use different skills one by one instead of having to manage many of them at the same time. That's why I think your first yoyo should be a responsive one.

Unresponsive Yoyo

The other type of yoyos are the unresponsive yoyos. They're called unresponsive because they don't get back to your hand even if you tug on the string, so you have to rewind the yoyo yourself every time you use it. That's why they're not the best option for beginners, you'd have to take the time to do it each time or learn some extra tricks that do it for you.

This type of yoyo is a better choice for experienced yoyoers who already know some of those tricks that rewind the yoyo without you having to do it. Those tricks are called binds or binding techniques, and you just have to wind part of the string in the gap in the center of the yoyo to give it the strength it needs to go back up to your hand.

TIP: There are yoyos made of plastic, wood, metal, plastic/metal mixes, or even different types of metal in the same yoyo. Any responsive yoyo is a good option to start with, but I recommend that you use a plastic one instead of any other material, especially metal. The reason is that when we're learning we may drop it more often and we can damage things around us or hurt ourselves with a metal yoyo, the plastic ones are usually lighter and also easier to handle.

Finding the Right Yoyo Shape

As I said at the beginning of this section, all yoyos may look extremely similar, but there are actually many different yoyos. You already know that there are responsive and unresponsive yoyos, but what about their shape?

Yoyos can come in many different shapes and those shapes affect the way they move, so you're going to need one type or another depending on the style of play and the tricks you want to learn.

Each shape has its own strengths and weaknesses, so there are three basic shapes and a whole range that combine or modify a little those three major shapes. Let's hear about the three basic shapes of yoyos: butterfly yoyos, classic or imperial yoyos, and modified or pinwheel yoyos.

Butterfly Yoyos

If you look at a butterfly yoyo from the front, you'll see that the outer edges of the disks are larger than the inner edges. The general shape of the yoyo can be a little more rounded or more V-shaped, but it will always remind you of the wings of a butterfly, that's where its name comes from. The outer sides of the disks can be either flat or curved inward. This is what a butterfly yoyo looks like:

Butterfly yoyos are perfect for string tricks because they have a fairly large gap in the middle, but for this very reason and because they're heavier on their outer edges they're not very good for loops.

So in general, butterfly yoyos are perfect for beginners and string tricks, which are also the first and easiest to learn, as you will see in a little while. However, for tricks involving loops it's better if you choose another yoyo shape.

Classic or Imperial Yoyos

Classic or imperial yoyos are, as its name suggests, the classic yoyos with a rounded shape that you see most of the time and that most of us have had at some point. Their inner sides are flat and their outer sides are a little curved, which gives them a more rounded overall shape. A classic or imperial yoyo is probably the first image that comes to your mind when you think of a yoyo, this is what they look like:

Yoyos with this shape are not good at string tricks because they have a pretty small gap in the middle, which makes it harder to line up the yoyo and the string so everything falls into place.

However, they're very good at loopings, so it might be a good idea to use a classic or imperial yoyo instead of a butterfly yoyo for some of the tricks you'll learn later in this book, like Around the World and Loop the Loop.

Flywheel or Modified Yoyos

Flywheel or modified yoyos are similar to classic or imperial yoyos, but the space between the two disks can be even narrower. The disks have both flat sides and curved edges, giving each individual disk a rounded shape. This is what a modified yoyo looks like:

They're very good at looping and spinning for a long time, but you can also use them for some simple string tricks despite their narrow gap. Although it can be used for those simple tricks, it's better to leave this type of yoyos for more advanced players.

What About the Right String Length?

Before you start playing with your yoyo, the last step is to find the correct string length for you, which basically depends on your height. In this step you will have to cut the string with scissors, so you can ask an adult for help if you need it. You can do it yourself, but be very careful!

Here's what you need to do to make sure your yoyo's string is the right size:

1. Completely unwind the entire string, untying it from the gap in the middle of the yoyo.

2. Make a loop with the string and tie a knot around the middle finger of your hand.

3. Place the hand with the string at the height of your belly button and let the string fall in front of you.

4. The yoyo should go down to about the height of your ankle, so you should cut the thread a little lower, almost at the point where it touches the ground. That extra length is for the loop you have to make to attach it again to the yoyo.

5. Tie the end of the string opposite your hand to the gap in the middle of the yoyo and you're ready to play!

If all went well, you now have a yoyo with the correct length to learn amazing tricks. In any case, test it by placing your hand at the height of your belly button and if you see that the yoyo reaches below your ankle, then you left too much string for the loop and you should cut a little more. I recommend that you cut little by little because you can always cut a little more, but if you go too far you will have a yoyo that's too short.

Types of Yoyo Play

There are an endless number of tricks you can do with your yoyo, but depending on the type and shape of your yoyo, you can do some tricks or others. This is why there are many styles of yoyo play, each with their own tricks. All those styles are divided into 5 main categories, although many of them have sections and some of them overlap with others.

These are the most important styles of play:

- 1A: Tricks are always performed with or even on the string. In this book you will learn some 1A style tricks, so we will see more about them in the next section.

- 2A: Tricks are performed with two yoyos, one in each hand.

- 3A: This is a mix of the two previous styles, you need two yoyos, one in each hand, to perform tricks on the strings.

- 4A: This style is also called offstring because all the tricks in this category are performed without the yoyo being tied to the string.

- 5A: This style is also called freehand because one end of the string is tied to the yoyo as usual, but the other end is tied to a small bouncy ball or something similar instead of your hand.

1A

In the 1A or single A style, as you already know, the tricks are always performed with or even on the string. Although it's common to start with a single responsive yoyo, more experienced players can do these tricks with an unresponsive yoyo as well. This is the best style of play for beginners and is often the first one new players learn because its tricks are the simplest and easiest to master.

Within the 1A style of play you can find different types of tricks:

- Loops and Regenerations: In these tricks you don't need to catch your yoyo and throw it again when it stops spinning because the tricks themselves will make it spin faster on its own.

- String Tricks: In this type of trick, as its name says, the main character is the string. The yoyo spins and rests on the string, those positions in which the yoyo is sitting on the string are called 'mounts'. The moves to go from one mount to the next are called 'transitions'.

- Picture Tricks: They're basically string tricks, but the difference here is that the yoyo doesn't end up mounted on the string, but hanging off the end of it. The magic here is that you can make amazing images with the string.

- Grinds: These are tricks where the yoyo is in contact with some part of your body or another object at the same time it's spinning.

- Slack String Tricks: These are also string tricks, but the most important difference here is that the string is not left taut, but instead is left loose to make, for example, loops.

Beginning at the Basics

Winding Your Yoyo

What's the first thing you have to do before playing with your yoyo? Exactly, wind the string! Winding all the string in the middle gap correctly may seem like a walk in the park, but trust me, it can also be trickier than it sounds.

You can just wrap the string around the middle gap without pulling on it too much and it will work fine most of the time, but... What happens if, when trying to wind it, the end of the string that's tied to the yoyo starts spinning around the bar between the disks instead of winding around it? Well, follow these steps to get it right:

1. Hold your yoyo in one hand and place your thumb just above the gap.

2. Take the string with your other hand and loop it around the gap, making sure to pull it tight above your finger. Tight enough that it's not a much bigger loop than it would be if you weren't using your finger, but not so much that you won't be able to pull your thumb out later.

3. Go around the gap a couple more times, but this time bring the string under your thumb.

4. Carefully pull out your thumb.

5. Keep winding the string as normal until it's all wound up.

If all goes well, which I'm sure it will, you're almost ready to throw your yoyo for the first time. And I say almost because you still need to learn the best way to hold it so that it doesn't slip out of your hand and your tricks turn out great.

How to Hold and Throw Your Yoyo

Once you've wound your yoyo, what's the next step? That's it! Now's the time to learn how to hold it correctly so you can throw it well.

The first thing you need to do is hold the yoyo in the palm of your dominant hand. Just in case you're wondering, your dominant hand is the one you do most things with, it's easy to tell if you think about which hand you write with, that's the one! From now on we will call that hand the yoyo hand.

Then you have to place the loop on the free end of the string around the middle finger of your yoyo hand. It's important that it's tied around your middle finger so that it's more or less in the center of the hand and you can hold it more comfortably. Make sure the loop isn't too tight, but tight enough to keep the yoyo from flying out of your hand when you throw it.

You will want to place the loop right in the middle of your finger, halfway between your knuckle and your fingernail. With the yoyo in the palm of your hand, the string should go from your middle finger to the top of the yoyo, as you can see in the drawing below.

Note that the string has a certain angle from the finger to the top of the yoyo, it doesn't lie directly on your hand.

Now that you have the yoyo wound and correctly placed in your yoyo hand, it's time to throw it!

First, bring your arm completely straight out in front of you with the palm of your yoyo hand facing up, and slightly close your hand on the yoyo, making sure your middle finger rests in the gap on the yoyo over the string.

Then bend your elbow up until the yoyo is almost up to your shoulder and fully stretch your arm out again. It's at this point that you should release the yoyo and let it slide over the tips of your fingers. As soon as the yoyo starts to unwind, quickly turn your yoyo hand so that your palm is facing down, and you can pick up the yoyo as it's winding back up.

Some of the tricks you're going to learn in this book will start holding and throwing the yoyo like you just learned, but some tricks are a little special and you'll have to throw the yoyo in a different way. But don't worry, everything will be perfectly ex-plained for you!

This is the standard way, so to speak, of throwing the yoyo, but as you get more confident with your yoyo and how to throw it, you'll be able to lower your arm a bit or bend your elbow a little less when releasing the yoyo. You can do whatever works for you because the important thing in the end is that you're comfortable.

Winding the string… check! Holding the yoyo… check! Throwing it… check! Ok, now that you know how to do all these things we can move on to the next section to learn a bunch of cool tricks, are you ready? Let's go!

Tricks Galore

One of the best things about yoyos is that they're not just toys, they're much more than that. Knowing that you have endless possibilities and that just by practicing you can get better and better at it every day makes it one of the best and most fun toys in the world.

In this section you will see a few tricks, starting with the basics and then moving on to more and more difficult tricks, but don't worry, it's just a matter of practice and repeating them over and over again will make you become an expert!

You may think that the first tricks are nothing special or fun, but trust me, they're the building blocks you need to be able to perform other really impressive tricks. It's important to master those building blocks perfectly, so give yourself as much time as you need to do that.

Before we start learning all these cool tricks, let me introduce you to an expression that you're going to see a lot from now on: 'make a quick tug'. This means that you have to give your yoyo string a quick, hard pull with your yoyo hand, but without lifting that hand or arm.

Ready to dive into this new world? Let the fun begin!

Throw Down

This trick is almost exactly the same as the yoyo throwing you just learned at the end of the previous section. Both this trick and the one you're going to learn right next will be pretty useful for many of the tricks you're going to learn so practice as much as you need, there's no rush!

The difference with the throw that you already saw, is that at the end of this trick you must catch the yoyo again with the hand that you threw it with. Pay attention!

Steps:

1. Bring your arm out in front of you with the palm of your yoyo hand facing up, and slightly close your hand on the yoyo, making sure your middle finger rests in the gap over the string.

2. Bend your elbow until the yoyo is almost up to your shoulder.

3. Fully stretch your arm out again, release the yoyo and let it slide over the tips of your fingers.

4. As soon as the yoyo starts to unwind, quickly turn your yoyo hand so that your palm is facing down.

5. When it's nearing the end of the string, make a quick tug upward on your yoyo, so it winds back up to your hand.

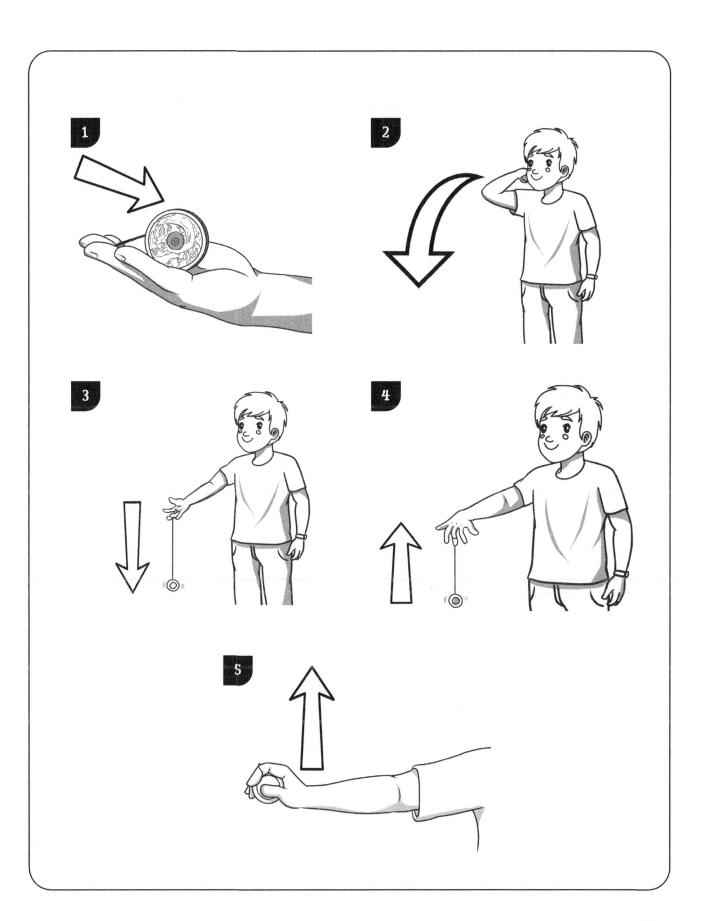

Gravity Pull

This trick is just another way to throw your yoyo, like the one you just learned about in the previous trick. Unlike the throw you've already seen, you don't have to actually throw the yoyo, instead gravity does all the work here. Many other tricks start with this way of throwing the yoyo so practice it as many times as you need until you master it.

There's a bit of confusion between this trick and the Throw Down you just saw, a lot of people mix them, but here's the key: the difference is that in the Throw Down you have to actively throw the yoyo down, while in the Gravity Pull (see its name?) is gravity that pulls the yoyo down without you doing anything to help it.

Steps:

1. Bring your arm out in front of you holding the yoyo in your hand, palm facing down.

2. Release the yoyo and let it unwind almost to the end of the string.

3. When it's nearing the end of the string, make a quick tug upward on your yoyo, so it winds back up to your hand.

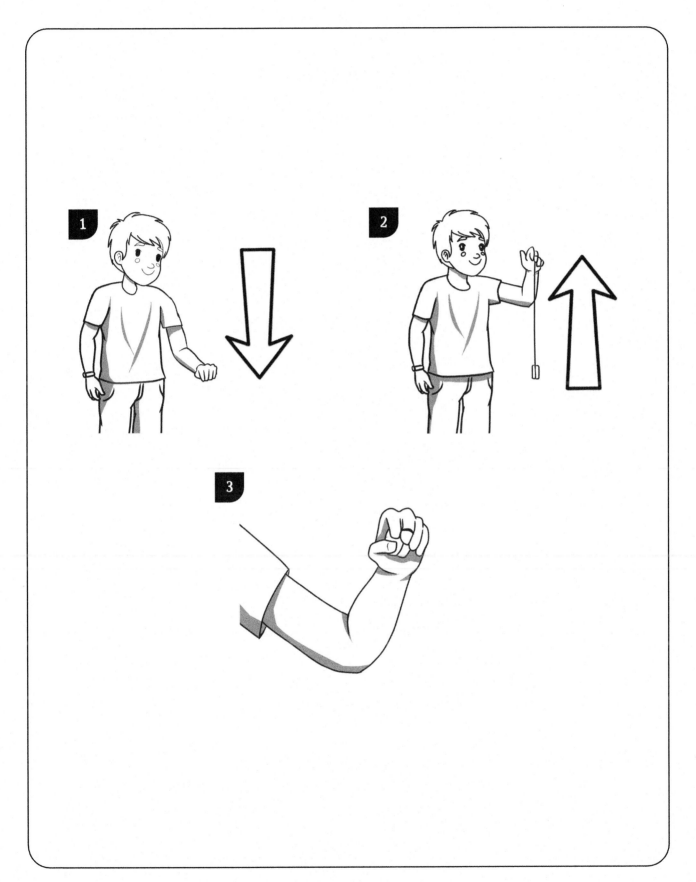

Sleeper

To be honest, the first tricks you learned were ways of throwing the yoyo rather than actual tricks. So this is the first trick where you will have to do more than just throw and catch the yoyo, and also many more complex tricks will have the Sleeper as part of their steps so take as long as you want and repeat until you do it perfect.

Steps:

1. Bring your arm out in front of you with the palm of your yoyo hand facing up, and slightly close your hand on the yoyo, making sure your middle finger rests in the gap over the string.

2. Bend your elbow until the yoyo is almost up to your shoulder.

3. Fully stretch your arm out again quickly to add speed to your yoyo, release it and let it slide over the tips of your fingers.

4. Let the yoyo unwind and spin at the end of the string for a few seconds. It's ok if you just count to 3 or even 5 in your head.

5. While the yoyo's still spinning, turn your yoyo hand so that your palm is facing down.

6. After those few seconds spinning, make a quick tug upward on your yoyo, so it winds back up to your hand.

As you can see, the Sleeper is just a Throw Down but giving the yoyo some time to spin before taking it back up. As you practice and get more confident with this trick, you will be able to let the yoyo spin longer and longer. Try it, I'm sure you can do it!

TIP: Make sure you throw your yoyo as straight down as you can so it spins longer, if you throw it at an angle it will stop spinning much sooner and you may not be able to get it back up into your hand.

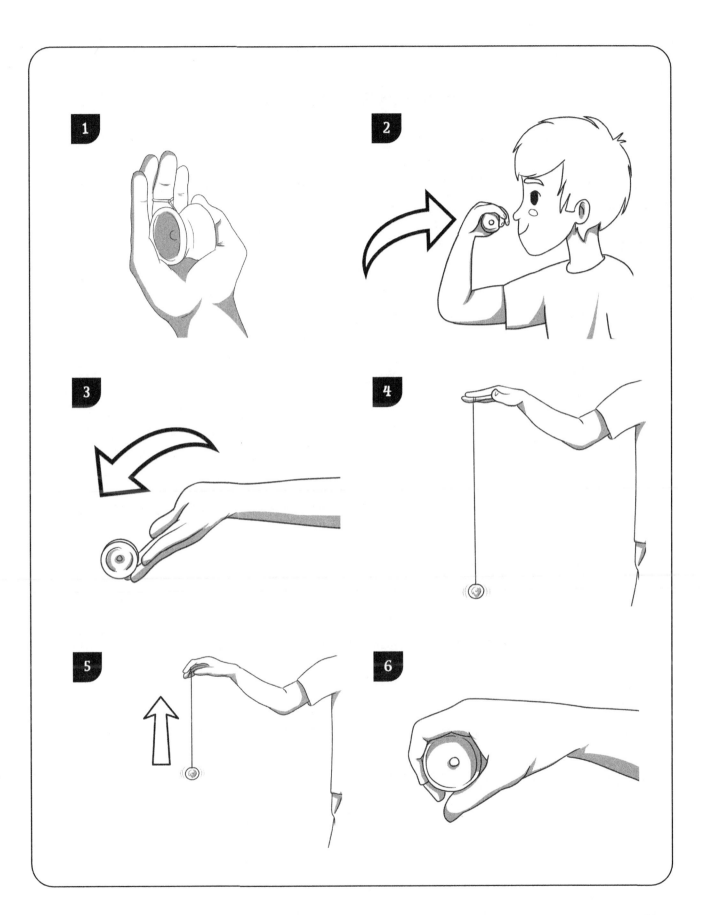

Reverse Sleeper

The Reverse Sleeper is basically the same as the Sleeper, the only difference is that you must flip your yoyo upside down before you throw it so that it spins in the opposite direction as in the previous trick. Go for it!

Steps:

1. Bring your arm out in front of you with the palm of your yoyo hand facing up, and slightly close your hand on the yoyo, making sure your middle finger rests in the gap over the string.

2. Now flip your yoyo upside down so that the string sits under the yoyo, touching your hand.

3. Bend your elbow up until the yoyo is almost up to your shoulder. Then fully stretch your arm out again quickly to add speed to your yoyo, release it and let it slide over the tips of your fingers.

4. Let the yoyo unwind and spin at the end of the string for a few seconds. It's ok if you just count to 3 or even 5 in your head.

5. While the yoyo's still spinning, turn your yoyo hand so that your palm is facing down.

6. After those few seconds spinning, make a quick tug upward on your yoyo, so it winds back up to your hand.

TIP: Make sure you throw your yoyo as straight down as you can so it spins longer, if you throw it at an angle it will stop spinning much sooner and you may not be able to get it back up into your hand.

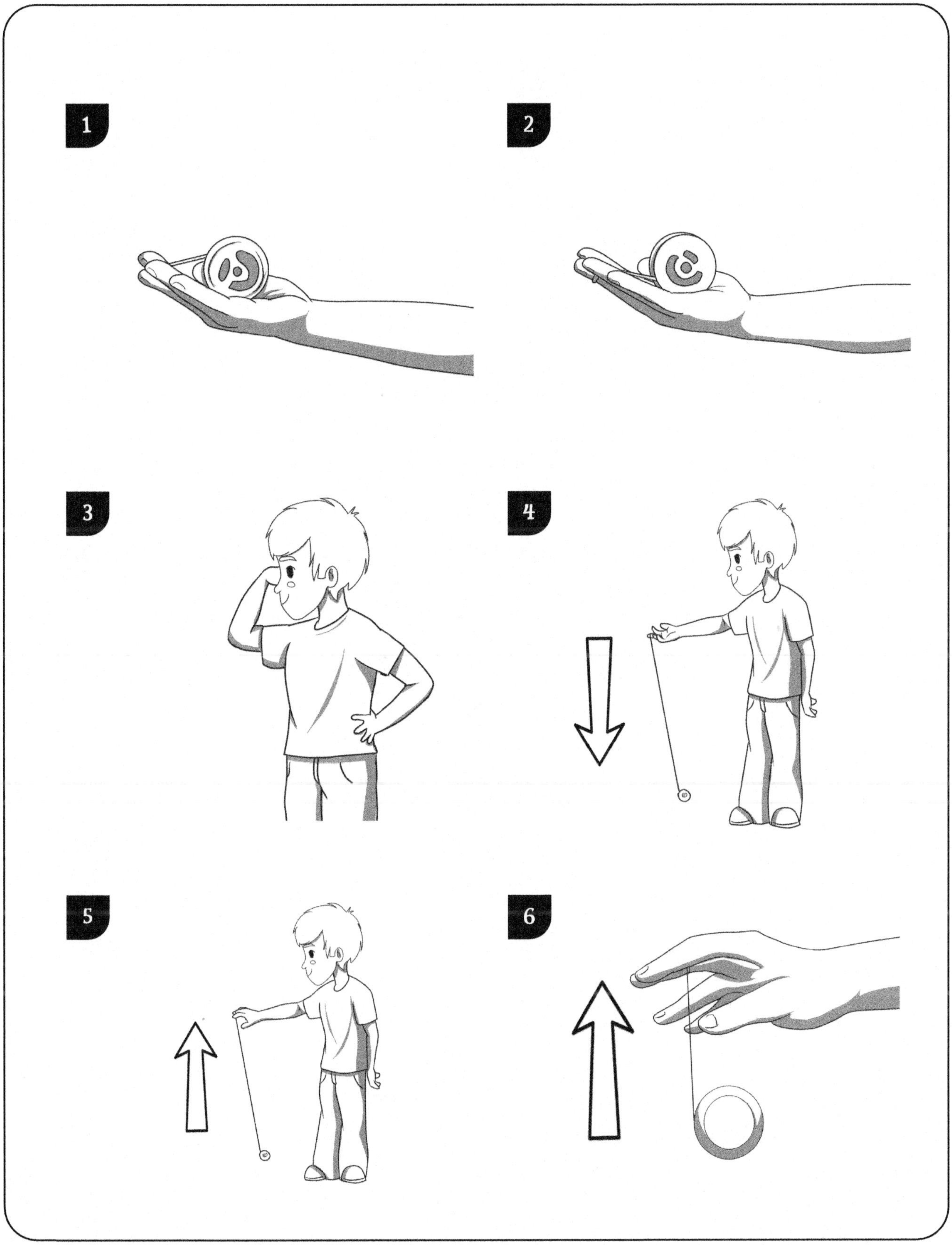
1
2
3
4
5
6

Forward Pass

Once you've practiced and mastered the first tricks of throwing the yoyo straight down, it's time to learn something a little different. How about we learn how to throw the yoyo forward and then catch it? This way of throwing your yoyo is also often repeated in many more complicated tricks so make sure you practice it a lot before moving on.

Steps:

1. Let your yoyo hand hang completely behind you with your palm facing back, and slightly close your hand on the yoyo, making sure your middle finger rests in the gap over the string.

2. Quickly throw your hand straight out in front of you and release the yoyo. Make sure your hand stays in the same position, if you do that you'll see that your hand's facing down when you release the yoyo.

3. Once the yoyo leaves your hand, flip it over so your palm is facing up and it's easier to catch it when it comes back.

4. When your yoyo's nearing the end of the string, make a quick tug upward on your yoyo, so it winds back up to your hand.

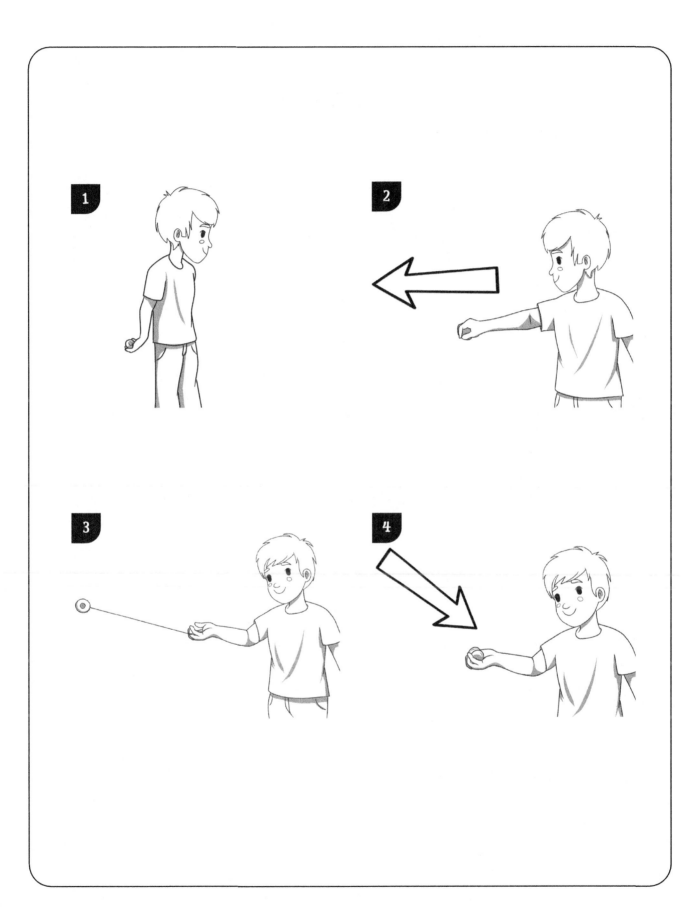

Breakaway

The Breakwaway is another way of throwing your yoyo, a little trickier than the ones you've learned so far because you have to throw your yoyo sideways. Many tricks where you need the yoyo to land on the string start with a throw like this one. It's okay if you don't get it right the first time, follow the steps one by one as many times as you need, I'm sure you'll master it in no time!

Steps:

1. Hold your yoyo in front of you, parallel to your body.

2. Raise your elbow until your arm ends up horizontal in front of you.

3. Quickly rotate your arm up and out, like you're making a circle. When your hand is reaching the bottom of that circle, release the yoyo toward the opposite side of your yoyo hand. For example, if your yoyo hand is your right hand, you should throw it toward the left side of your body.

4. Once the yoyo reaches the end of the string and spins in the air, make a quick tug on your yoyo to bring it back.

TIP: Be patient and give yourself as much time as you need to get it right. This is the hardest throw you'll learn in this book, but I know you can do it! Remember: timing is everything here, so practicing over and over until you know exactly when to release the yoyo is the key to this trick.

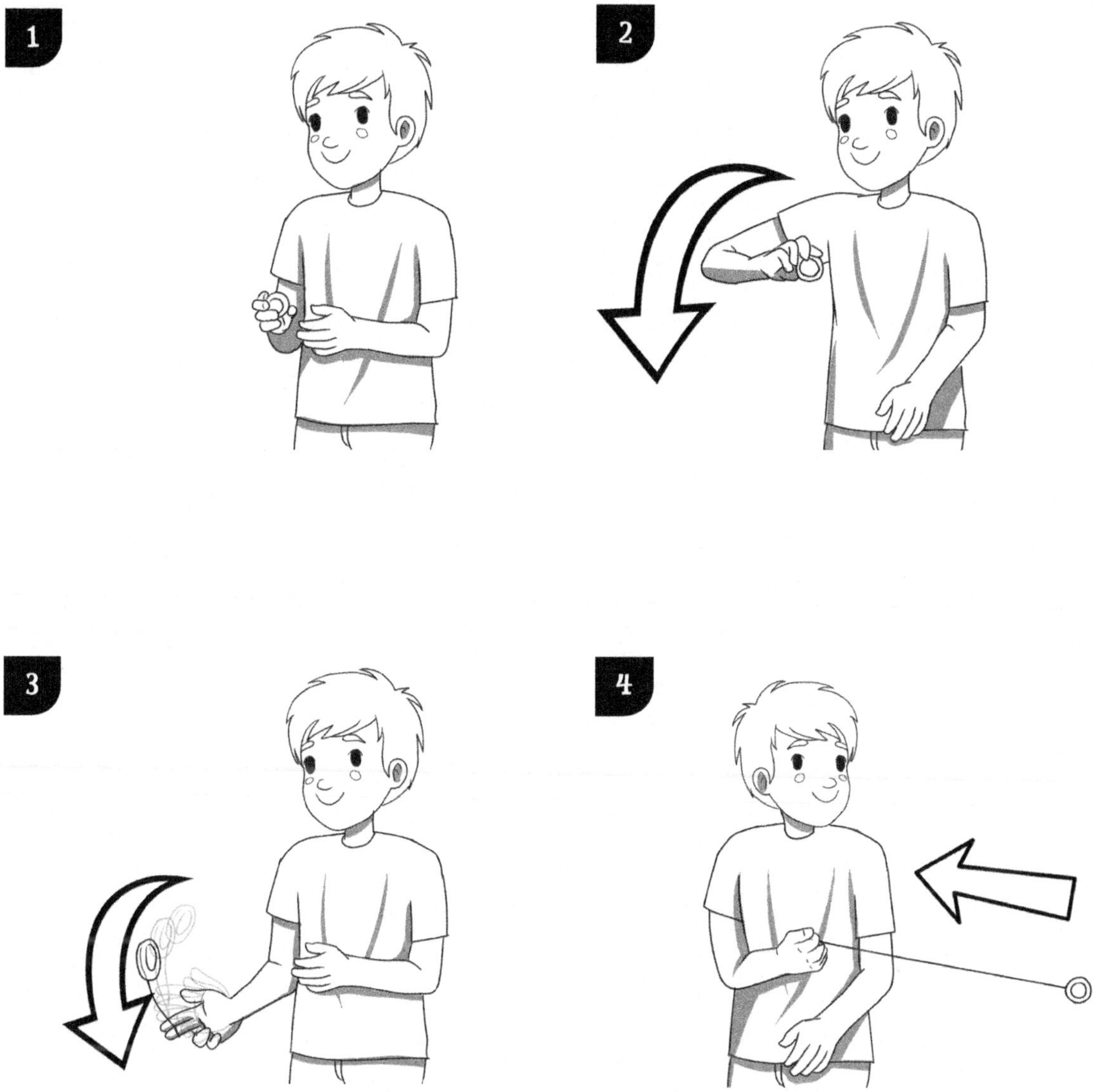
1
2
3
4

Walk the Dog

Walk the Dog is easily the most famous trick and one of the first tricks that new yoyo players learn. Walk the Dog belongs to the group of tricks called 'grinds', which as you already know are tricks where the yoyo is in contact with some part of your body or another object at the same time that it's spinning. It was actually the first grind ever, and here the yoyo spins on the floor, it 'walks' in front of you.

This trick starts out just like the Sleeper you learned a few pages back, but don't worry, here's all the information you need to make it perfect!

Steps:

1. Bring your arm out in front of you with the palm of your yoyo hand facing up, then bend your elbow until the yoyo is almost up to your shoulder.

2. Fully stretch your arm out again quickly to add speed to your yoyo, release it and let it slide over the tips of your fingers.

3. Slowly lower the yoyo until it touches the ground.

4. Since the yoyo's spinning pretty fast, you'll see that it moves forward on the ground, it 'walks' in front of you. You can even take a few steps with it!

5. After a few seconds walking, make a quick tug upward on your yoyo, so it winds back up to your hand. Touching the ground will stop your yoyo from spinning for a long time, so tug your yoyo sooner than you normally would.

TIP: The faster you throw your yoyo, the longer it will walk on the floor before you have to pull it back up.

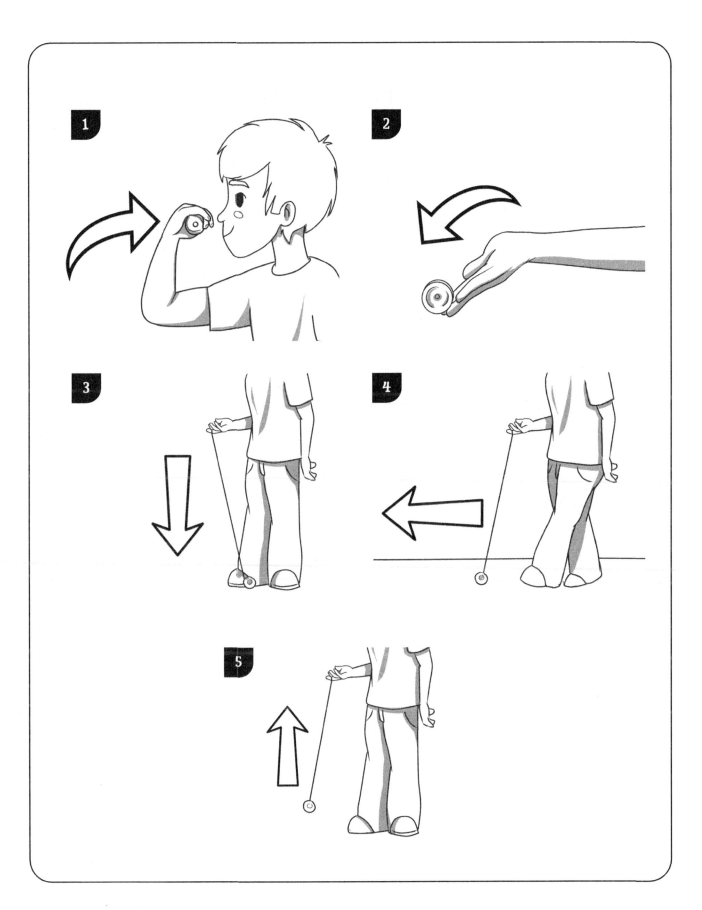

Walk the Cat

Do you remember what happened with the Sleeper and the Reverse Sleeper? Those tricks had the same moves, but in the Reverse Sleeper you had to hold your yoyo upside down. The same thing happens here between Walk the Dog and Walk the Cat: they have the same moves, but to get this very special cat to walk you have to hold your yoyo upside down too. Holding the yoyo like this will also make it roll on the ground in the opposite direction, walking backward toward you instead of forward.

Steps:

1. Bring your arm out in front of you with the palm of your yoyo hand facing up, then flip your yoyo upside down so that the string sits under the yoyo, touching your hand.

2. Bend your elbow until the yoyo is almost up to your shoulder, then fully stretch your arm out again quickly to add speed to your yoyo, release it and let it slide over the tips of your fingers.

3. Slowly lower the yoyo until it touches the ground.

4. Throwing the yoyo like this will make it spin backward, so it will start walking backward toward you instead of forward.

5. After a few seconds walking, make a quick tug upward on your yoyo, so it winds back up to your hand. Touching the ground will stop your yoyo from spinning for a long time, so tug your yoyo sooner than you normally would.

TIP: The faster you throw your yoyo, the longer it will walk on the floor before you have to pull it back up.

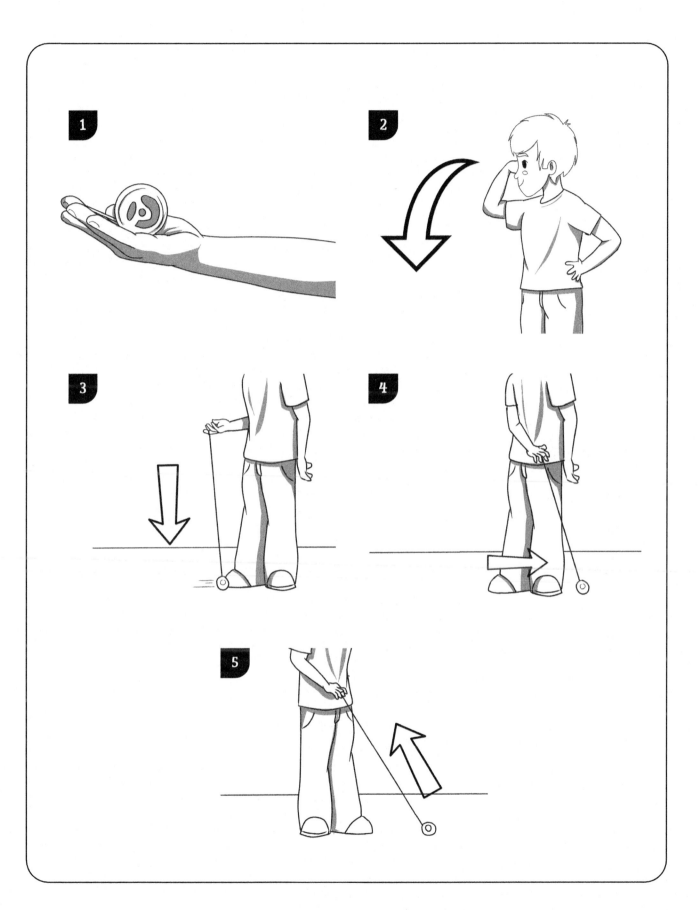

Over the Falls

This trick is a Forward Pass made harder. First you have to follow the same steps as in the Forward Pass and throw your yoyo in front of you, but this time you don't have to catch it when it comes back to you. Here you have to make it fall down over your hand instead and let it spin like in the Sleeper. It's easier than it sounds!

Steps:

1. Let your yoyo hand hang completely behind you with your palm facing back, and slightly close your hand on the yoyo, making sure your middle finger rests in the gap over the string.

2. Quickly throw your hand straight out in front of you and release the yoyo as you do so.

3. When your yoyo's nearing the end of the string, make a quick tug upward on your yoyo, so it winds back up to your hand.

4. Now, instead of catching the yoyo, pull your hand back and down almost to your hip. This will make the yoyo go over your wrist and fall right down toward the ground still spinning.

5. After a few seconds spinning in that position, make another quick tug upward on your yoyo so it winds back up to your hand, and catch it this time.

TIP: Timing is very important for this trick, so keep practicing over and over until you know exactly when to release the yoyo, and when to bring your hand back and down to your hip.

Around the World

Around the World is also one of the most famous yoyo tricks, right behind Walk the Dog. To make your yoyo travel Around the World you will have to throw it in front of you and then make it spin around your shoulder. You'll see that the first steps of this trick are the same as in the Forward Pass. Are you ready?

Steps:

1. Let your yoyo hand hang completely behind you with your palm facing back, and slightly close your hand on the yoyo, making sure your middle finger rests in the gap over the string.

2. Quickly throw your hand straight out in front of you and release the yoyo as you do so.

3. When the yoyo reaches the end of the string, instead of making a quick tug to get it back, pull it up to make it spin over your shoulder.

4. You can make up to 3 full circles around your shoulder.

5. 5. Slow down as the yoyo approaches the end of the last circle.

6. Once the yoyo is in the same position where it all started in front of you, make a quick tug upward on your yoyo, so it winds back up to your hand.

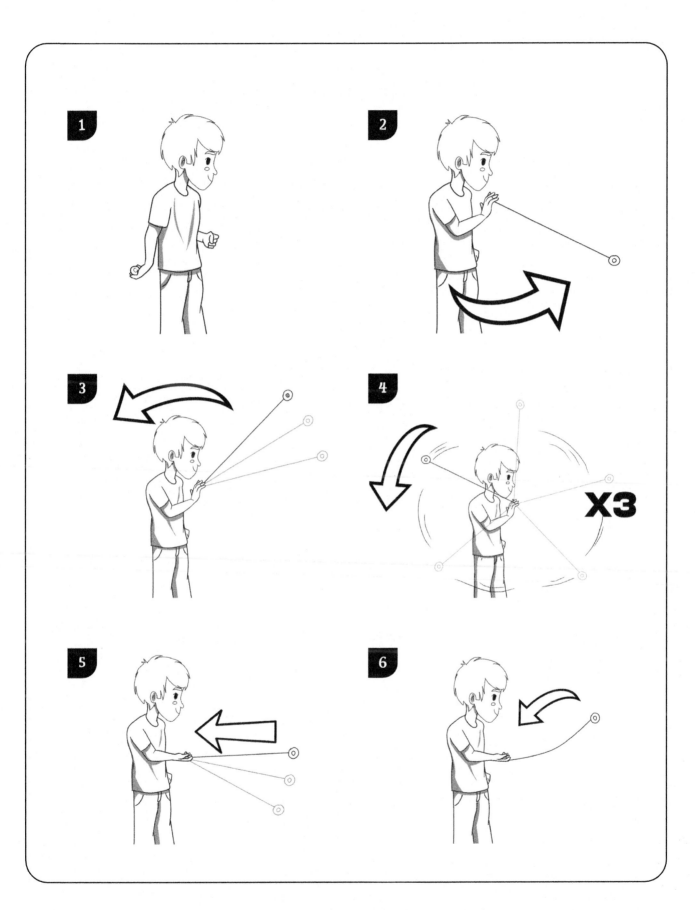

Around the Corner

This trick is quite simple, but it has something special that you will have to practice a few times until you get it right. That special something is that you won't see your yoyo all the time because part of the trick will be behind your arm, so you will have to learn to feel your yoyo. How do you do that? Like everything else in this book, try and try again until you master it!

Steps:

1. Bring your arm out in front of you with the palm of your yoyo hand facing up and bend your elbow until the yoyo is almost up to your shoulder. Then fully stretch it out again quickly to release your yoyo and let it slide over the tips of your fingers.

2. Let the yoyo unwind and spin at the end of the string, while you bend your elbow so that the yoyo goes behind your arm until it hangs over your shoulder. Make sure to do this really slowly so that your yoyo doesn't start swinging.

3. Bend your elbow down again to pull the yoyo up a bit. Don't worry, the yoyo can keep spinning even after hanging for a while.

4. Give the string a little tug so the yoyo goes over your shoulder and back toward your hand.

5. Don't catch your yoyo, let it go over your hand and fall down toward the ground, spinning at the end of the string like it does in the Sleeper.

6. After a few seconds spinning, make a quick tug upward on your yoyo, so it winds back up to your hand.

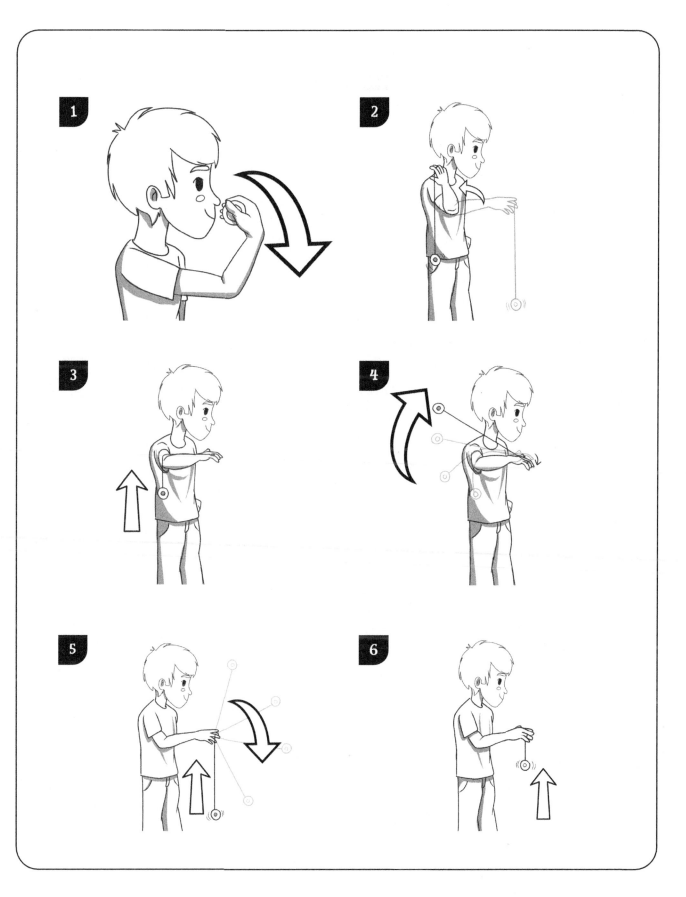

Tidal Wave

Tidal Wave is a simple, easy to learn trick that will come in handy when you're learning more advanced and complicated tricks. Be careful, though, as this will be the first trick so far that needs you to use both of your hands. While it may be difficult at first, I will keep it simple so that you can focus and get used to that feeling. From there, you will be a master in no time!

Steps:

1. Bring your arm out in front of you with the palm of your yoyo hand facing up and bend your elbow until the yoyo is almost up to your shoulder. Then fully stretch it out again quickly to release your yoyo and let it slide over the tips of your fingers, just like you would do in the Sleeper. Make sure to do it fast so the yoyo ends up spinning at the end of the string for a pretty long time.

2. Place your other hand right in front of your yoyo hand, with your index finger touching the string.

3. Slowly move that hand toward the end of the string, always touching it, until it's just a few inches away from the yoyo.

4. Tug the string lightly with that hand, while also making a tug with your yoyo hand at the same time to pull it back. This will make the yoyo go over your yoyo hand and make a full circle.

5. Once the yoyo has made the circle and it's in front of you again, make a quick tug upward on your yoyo, so it winds back up to your hand.

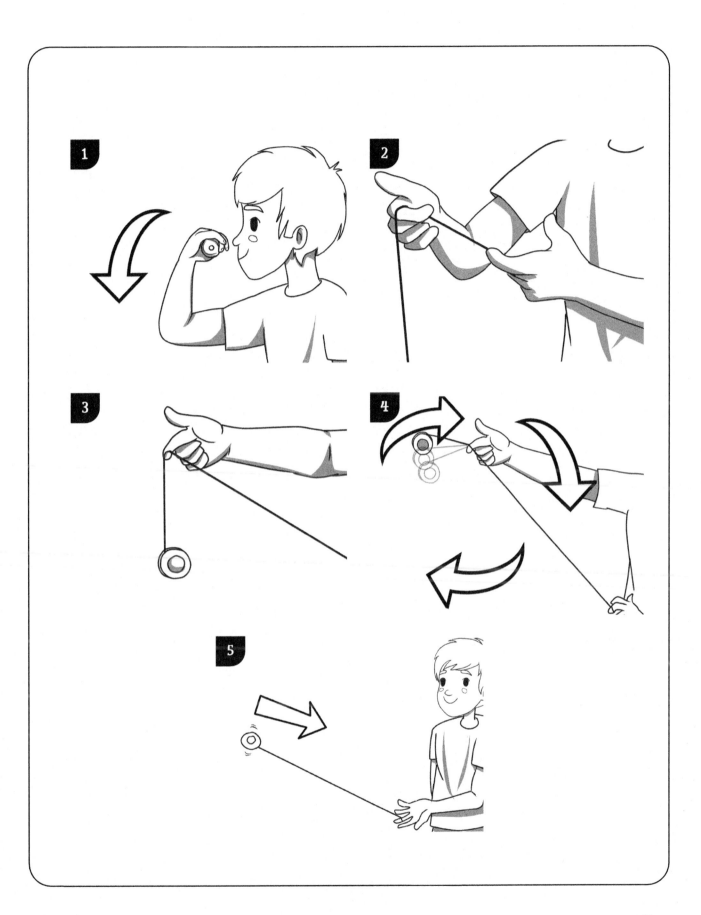

Pinwheels

There are a few different tricks called Pinwheels, so you may find different tricks under the same name if you search the internet or other books. Those tricks are essentially the same, but with some changes to the way you throw the yoyo or pinch the string that add difficulty depending on how advanced the player is. Here we're going to use what you just learned for the Tidal Wave to spin your yoyo like a helicopter. This trick is basically a Tidal Wave, but throwig your yoyo sideways instead of forward.

Steps:

1. Bring your arm out in front of you with the palm of your yoyo hand facing up and bend your elbow until the yoyo is almost up to your shoulder. Then fully stretch it out again quickly to release your yoyo and let it slide over the tips of your fingers, just like you would do in the Sleeper. Make sure to do it fast so the yoyo ends up spinning at the end of the string for a pretty long time.

2. Raise your yoyo hand a little, and use your other hand to pinch the string between your thumb and your index finger a few inches away from the yoyo.

3. Make sure to move both hands away from your body so that you won't get hurt when the yoyo starts spinning.

4. Now use the hand that's pinching the string to spin the yoyo in circles as many times as you like, just be careful not to hit anything with it.

5. To get the yoyo back you have two options:

   • Option #1 is to slow it down and make a quick tug on your yoyo when all the string and yoyo are horizontal, just like you would wind back the Breakaway.

   • Option #2 is to simply drop it so that it spins at the end of the string, like the Sleeper, and at that point make a quick tug upward on your yoyo, so it winds back up to your hand.

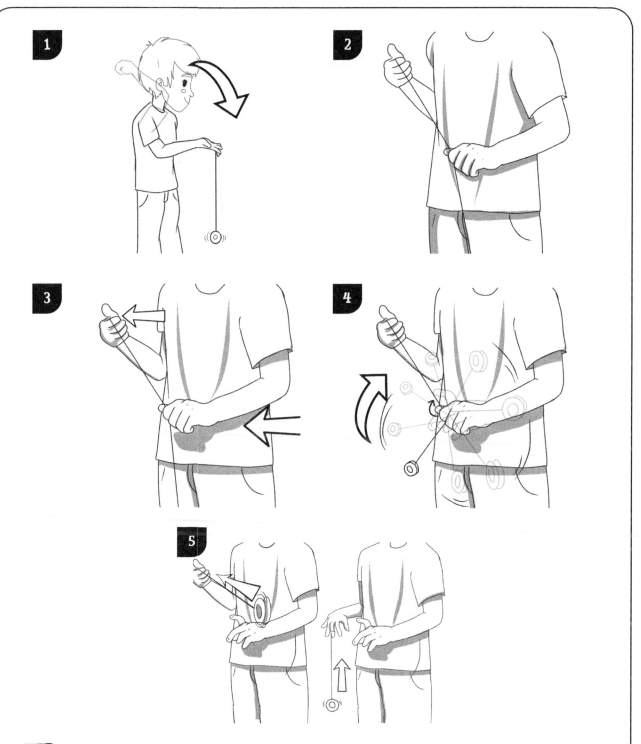

TIP: If you want to try a different way to start this trick, instead of throwing it like in the Sleeper, you can try throwing a Breakaway. That is, throw your yoyo horizontally to the side of your body opposite your yoyo hand and pinch the string while the yoyo is flying through the air in front of you.

Hop the Fence

Hop the Fence is a more advanced form of the Throw Down, but don't worry, advanced doesn't mean hard. It belongs to the group of tricks known as 'loops and regenerations'. Why? Because you're going to throw your yoyo over and over again without ever catching it so that it regains its speed or spins faster and faster every time. This trick's not the easiest to master, but it's the perfect training for the two tricks that you will see below so practice as many times as you need, take your time!

There's one thing you need to know even though you don't really need it right now, just in case it's useful for other tricks. As you do this trick, your yoyo string will get tighter if your yoyo hand is your right hand and looser if your yoyo hand is your left one.

Steps:

1. Bring your arm out in front of you with the palm of your yoyo hand facing up and bend your elbow until the yoyo is almost up to your shoulder. Then fully stretch it out again quickly to release your yoyo and let it slide over the tips of your fingers, just like you would do in the Throw Down.

2. Quickly turn your yoyo hand so that your palm is facing down, and make a quick tug upward on your yoyo, so it winds back up to your hand when it's nearing the end of the string.

3. Instead of catching it, when the yoyo's just a few inches away from your hand, bring your yoyo hand a little forward.

4. Bringing your hand forward will cause the yoyo to flip over your hand in a circle and fall back down toward the ground.

5. At this point you should repeat the process of making a quick tug, bringing your hand forward, and letting the yoyo flip over it to fall back down. If you want to make an amazing Hop the Fence you have do that at least 3 times and up to 10.

6. Once you're done, make a quick tug upward on your yoyo, so it winds back up to your hand, like you would in a regular Throw Down.

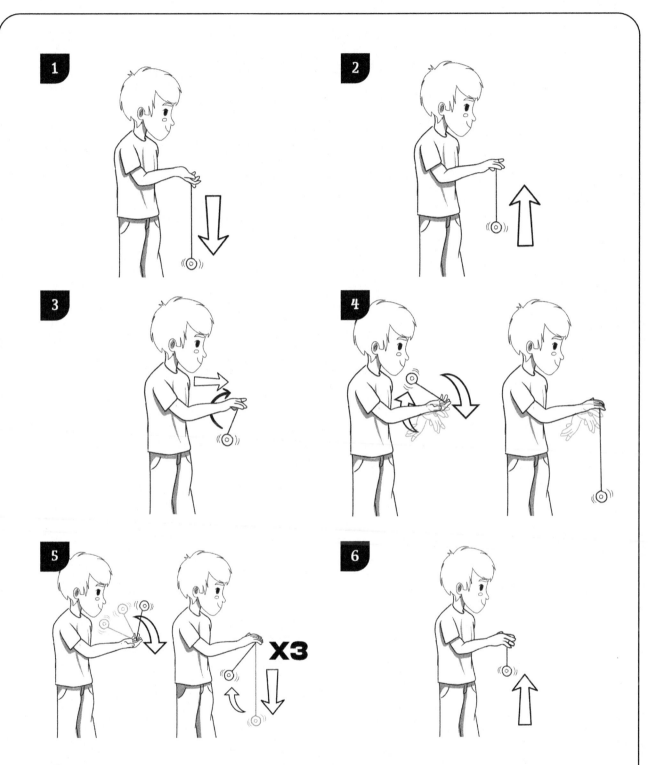

TIP: You can do this entire trick with your yoyo hand still, but you'll find it's easier to flip it a bit like following the motion of the yoyo as it flips around your hand.

Three-Leaf Clover

Remember a few tricks ago when you learned the Over the Falls? So let's give it a twist! A Three-Leaf Clover is a quite advanced trick, but in the end it's just a series of three Over the Falls in a row: the first one a little upward, the second one straight in front of you, and the third one exactly like the trick you already learned. Forget about four-leaf clovers, I'm sure this Three-Leaf Clover will be your lucky one!

Steps:

1. Let your yoyo hand hang completely behind you with your palm facing back, as you'd do in the Over the Falls trick that you already know, and quickly throw your hand out in front of you to release the yoyo, only here you have to throw it slightly upward.

2. When your yoyo reaches the end of the string, make a quick tug upward on your yoyo so it winds back to you, and at the same time pull your hand down a bit, until it's completely straight in front of you, as it would be in a regular Over the Falls. This will make your yoyo flip over your hand in a circle.

3. As the yoyo flips be ready to lower your hand another little bit just as the yoyo is right in front of you. This will make your yoyo flip over your hand again.

4. This time be ready to pull your hand back and down almost to your hip. This will make the yoyo go over your wrist and fall right down toward the ground still spinning, like the Sleeper.

5. This makes a total of 3 flips around your hand so you can make a quick tug upward on your yoyo now, so it winds back up to your hand.

TIP: Don't be afraid that your yoyo will stop spinning halfway through the trick, you don't need to do it extremely fast so that the yoyo doesn't lose its speed. Remember that flips go from higher to lower so gravity will be your friend here and will help you maintain the speed of your yoyo.

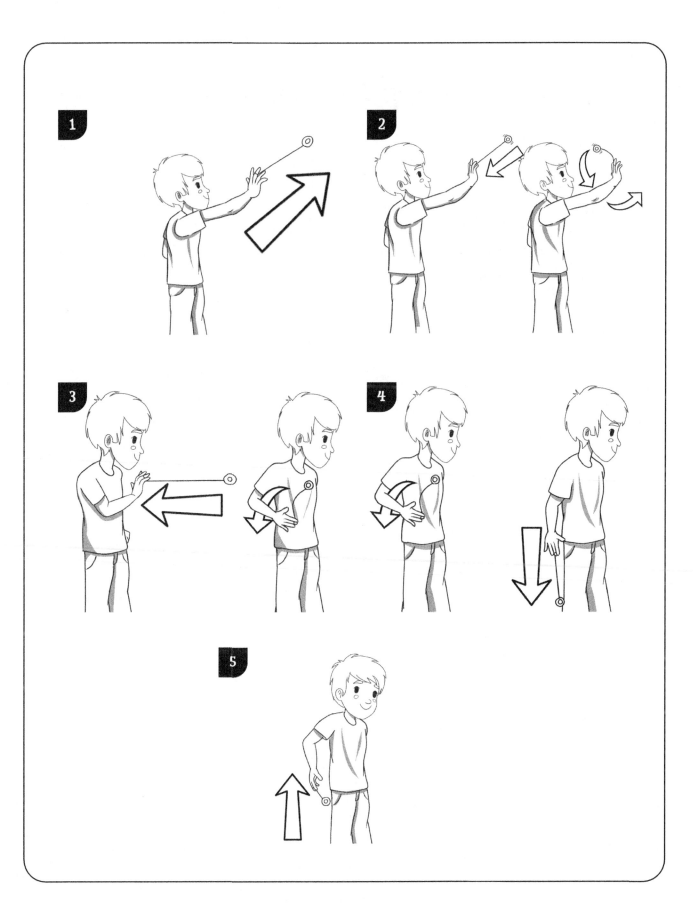

Loop the Loop

Loop the Loop is very similar to the Three-Leaf Clover trick, but there is one small detail that makes it a bit harder: this time you won't have gravity to help you. In the Loop the Loop trick you have to do three Over the Falls in a row too, but this time all three throws are right in front of you, always at the same height. There's no shortcuts here, the key to getting it right is practice, practice, and... did I say practice?

Steps:

1. Let your yoyo hand hang completely behind you with your palm facing back, as you'd do in the Over the Falls trick that you already know, and quickly throw your hand out in front of you to release the yoyo.

2. When your yoyo's nearing the end of the string, make a quick tug upward on your yoyo so it winds back, and pull your hand back and down almost to your hip, this will make the yoyo go over your wrist.

3. At this point, don't let the yoyo fall down toward the ground, use its speed to throw it forward again instead.

4. Pull the yoyo back to you again and bring your hand down almost to your hip so that the yoyo goes over your wrist once more. Repeat this same step as many times as you like, but a good Loop the Loop should have at least three yoyo flips.

5. After the last flip, make a quick tug on your yoyo, so it winds back to your hand.

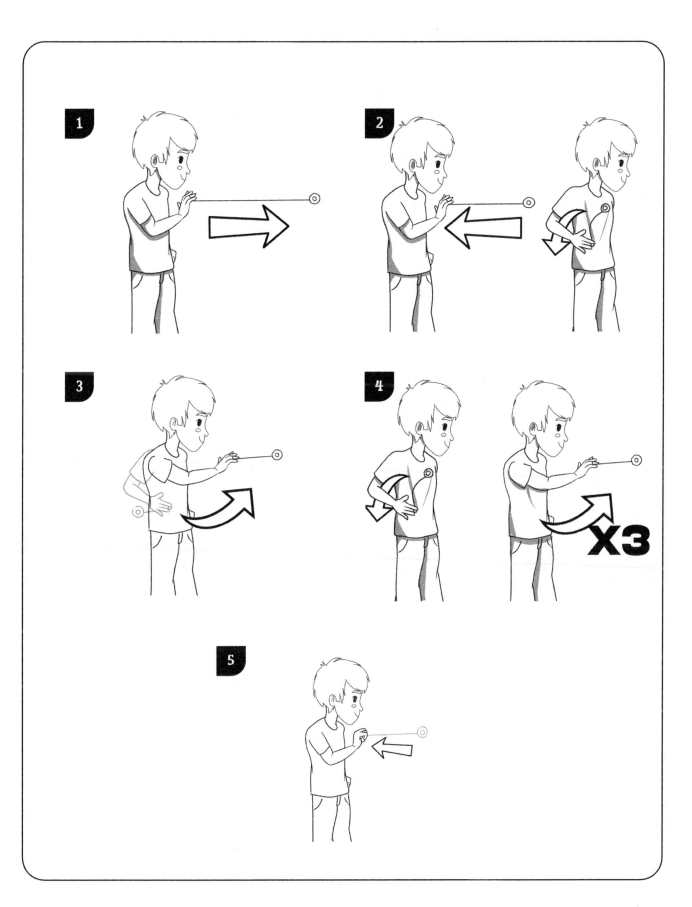

Sleeping Beauty

The Sleeping Beauty is considered one of the basic techniques of yoyoing because it allows you to unravel the string whenever you need to. When you do a lot of flips and loops in a row, the string can get quite messy and that can end up messing up the whole trick. With the Sleeping Beauty you're going to fix all that while doing a super cool trick that will amaze your friends and family.

Steps:

1. With your arm straight out in front of you, throw your yoyo sideways so that it ends up spinning parallel to the ground as it falls down. It's like a sideways Sleeper.

2. As your yoyo nears the end of the string, hook your thumb halfway down the string and pull it up until both your hands are about the same height.

3. When both hands are at the same height, you will see the string spin out over the top of your yoyo. Let it spin like this for a few seconds.

4. Once the string's done spinning, push the string up with your thumb so that the yoyo floats in the air for a moment.

5. Make a quick tug on your yoyo to get it back, just like you would wind back the Breakaway.

There's a very similar trick called the Flying Saucer that you can use to do exactly the same, fix messy strings. The only difference is that you don't have to lift the string with your thumb, but let the yoyo fall toward the ground after throwing it sideways and put your hand right on top of it to let the string spin out over your yoyo. After spinning for a few seconds, you have to pull the yoyo up and once it's parallel to your yoyo hand, make a quick tug so it winds back to you. It's called a Flying Saucer or UFO because the way the yoyo spins, parallel to the ground, makes it look from outer space.

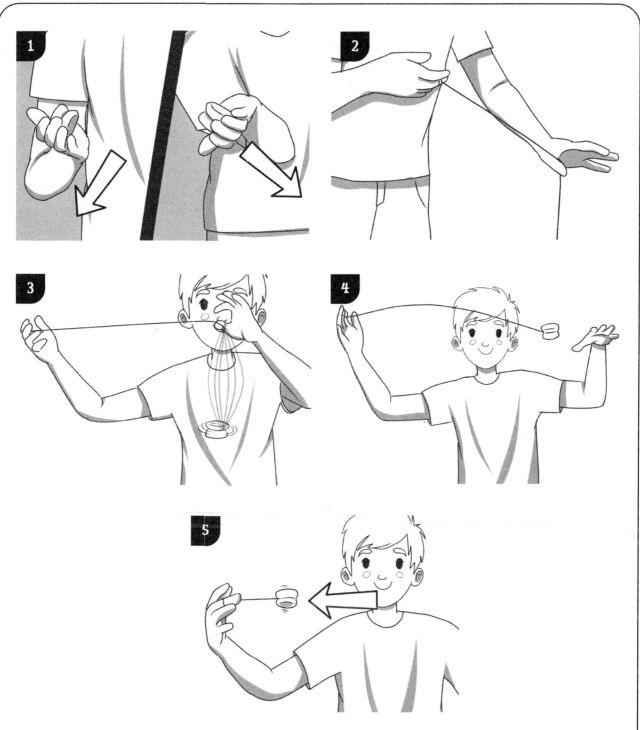

TIP: As you do any of these tricks, your yoyo string will get tighter if you throw it to your right, and looser if you throw it to your left. Since you may need to throw your yoyo to either side, it's important to practice throwing it both ways.

Fast Wind Up

The Fast Wind Up is is probably the trick that you will use the most of all the ones you've learned so far. This trick will help you wind your yoyo much faster and easier than winding the string around the yoyo yourself. This will be super useful if you decide to try an unresponsive yoyo, but even if you use a responsive yoyo all the time it's likely that it will end up unwinding more than once, so this trick will also work for you in those cases. Why is this cool, useful trick near the end of the book instead of the beginning? Well, because it helps you wind the string faster, but it's not an easy trick so it was important that you learn other things and get confident with your yoyo first.

Steps:

1. Hold your yoyo with the string fully unwound a little above your head.

2. Now take your other hand and place it on top of the yoyo, with the string between your middle and ring fingers.

3. While holding the yoyo with the string between your fingers, pull the string as far as you can to make it as taut as possible.

4. Now, at the same time, pull your yoyo hand up while bringing your other hand down, spinning the yoyo with your fingers.

5. Quickly lower your yoyo hand and you'll see the yoyo winding up.

6. It probably won't wind all the way up, so you'll have to manually wind the piece of string left, it shouldn't be too long.

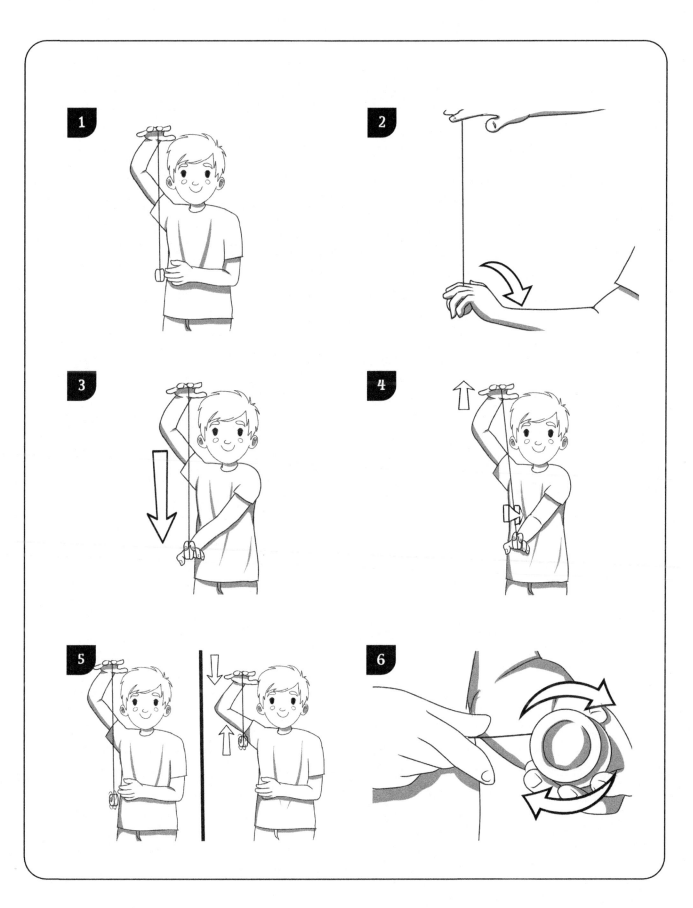

Rock the Baby

Rock the Baby is another one of the most famous tricks you can do with a yoyo and arguably one of the most iconic, it's definitely one of the most impressive tricks that are still easy to learn. It belongs to the group of tricks called 'picture tricks' because it's more than just throwing and catching the yoyo, it's about making figures with it. This is the first trick you'll learn where you're going to have to move both hands at the same time so I'll try to make the instructions as clear as possible. And you know… practice makes perfect!

Steps:

1. Bring your arm out in front of you with the palm of your yoyo hand facing up, bend your elbow until the yoyo is almost up to your shoulder, and fully stretch it out again to release your yoyo, just like you would do in the Sleeper. Make sure to do it fast so the yoyo ends up spinning at the end of the string for a pretty long time.

2. Bring your yoyo hand up to the height of your head, and place your other hand around the string, just a few inches below your yoyo hand.

3. Bring that other hand up until that part of the string ends up at the height of your head as well.

4. Now bring your yoyo hand down and grab the string a few inches above the yoyo.

5. Bring your yoyo hand back up so that both hands are at the same height again.

6. Spread the fingers of your other hand as far as you can to separate the string on both sides as much as you can. Everything will be fine for now if you've managed to make a triangle with the string..

7. Keep your yoyo hand in the same position and place your other hand just below it, so the yoyo ends up inside the triangle. Make sure to keep both hands far enough apart that the string doesn't hang loose on the sides of the triangle.

8. To make this trick even more special, push your yoyo with your yoyo hand so it moves back and forth inside the string triangle. Now you're rocking your baby!

9. Carefully let go of the string from both hands so the yoyo falls down toward the ground, and make a quick tug upward on your yoyo, so it winds back up to your hand.

TIP: When you're learning picture tricks, the biggest problem new players have is that it's hard to follow all the steps to make the figure while keeping the yoyo spinning all the way to the end. That's why it's a great idea to start by learning how to make the figure, just the figure, without your yoyo spinning. Let it hang in front of you until it stops spinning, saving you all that anxiety and frustration if the yoyo stops spinning halfway through the trick. Once you've mastered all the steps, you can start spinning the yoyo a little faster each time until you get a perfect trick.

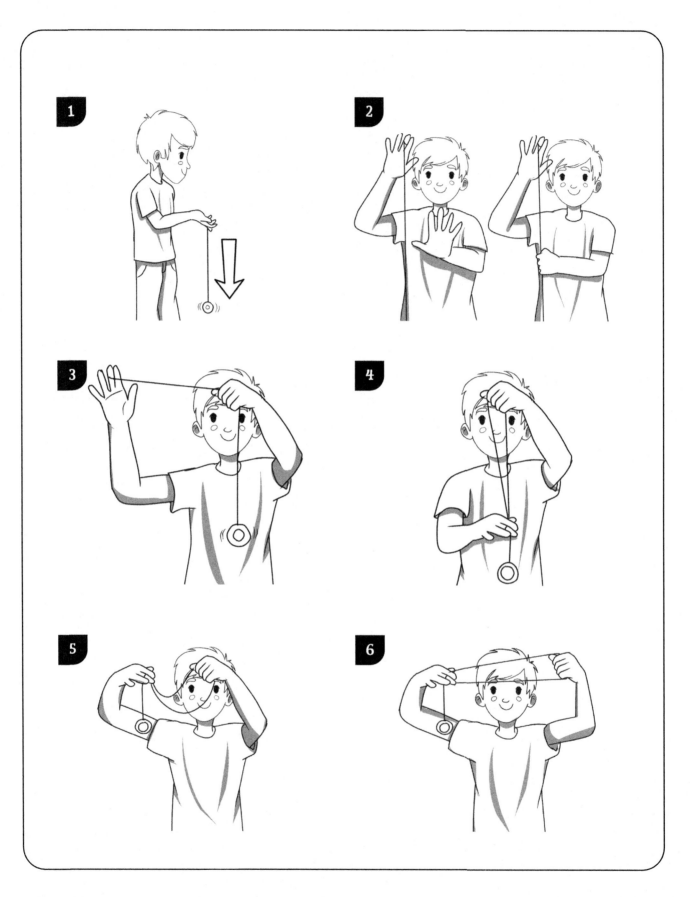

7

8

9

Conclusion

A yoyo may seem like an extremely simple toy, but they offer us endless possibilities: we can use a yoyo in hundreds of different ways, you can't count how many tricks there are, you can even mix this and that step to create new, incredible tricks!

I hope you had a blast with this book, I certainly had a lot of fun writing it and I hope it gives you hours and hours of fun too. Now it's your turn to leave your friends and family speechless with all these amazing yoyo tricks. I'm sure you're a great yoyoer now!

Remember, even if this book is meant to challenge you with increasingly complex tricks, the ultimate goal is always to have fun. Don't forget that and… who knows? Maybe the next yoyo world champion is reading this book right now!

Printed in Great Britain
by Amazon

29095993R00037